Snippets

Dr. Brendell Thomas Francis

ISBN 978-1-0980-8163-8 (paperback)
ISBN 978-1-0980-8164-5 (digital)

Christian Faith Publishing, Inc.
832 Park Avenue
Meadville, PA 16335
www.christianfaithpublishing.com

All Scripture references are from the KING JAMES VERSION unless otherwise stated.

Printed in the United States of America

Within Snippets you will find inspirational messages, motivational words that can cause you to think about your life and how you can proceed to change. It's designed to inspire you from a state of despair and hopefully give you a new vision of hope. Open at any page and enjoy.

I believe that God gave me these words of inspiration which I have shared with individual people and with groups. I hope you enjoy them as much as others.

Acknowledgments

I would like to thank my brothers, James A. Thomas Jr. and John E. Thomas, who supported me by speaking prophetically into my life. I want to thank all my family members near and far who have loved me no matter what! And to all my many friends who I have met over the years who took time out of their own lives to bring that special something to my life. And to those new friends who will get their opportunity to explore and experience the power of God just by reading these inspirational words here in this book. God will transform anyone, anywhere, and at any time, using every available tool. So gain as much as you can here, then go on to your "next"!

My Life, My Truth

I Was a Forgotten Woman That Escaped

I want to introduce to you my evidence of God rescuing me. I, who was truly prepared and predestined for his purposes. I have been contemplating on where should I begin telling my story, my life.

It was in the middle of the night when I decided to go out at night. My parents were asleep from a drunken stupor. I wasn't sure how, so I planned it. I barely opened the top of the hinges and could hardly push the window up. I was only six years old and my strength was not there. So I kept at it until I saw the way outside. It was very dark but the one streetlight was lit. I sat on the porch on that cool night, and I knew I had to come back inside because it was a chilling nighttime. But I began looking out the window and then going out my bedroom window. I liked going to school, so when I went out, I even wanted to come back in time to get some sleep. I went to school. I liked going to school; my teachers kept including me in activities. My nightlife became my wonderland. The moon and stars lit up the night sky and was adventurous. I just wanted to know the night scene. The night scene had music and people you didn't see in the morning. I would follow the sounds of the night. There were houses that let people come by all times of the night. My father left money in his pants pocket and I just needed a quarter. That quarter in my day brought me lots of cookies and candy. I was thinking about how good I felt and not scared to go outside at night. People in my day didn't bother children because they were doing their things: playing "spades," a card game, or just drinking hometown homemade brew. The lady that own the store lived within the store and she was in a wheelchair, so I began sitting in her store at night. She was always there. Sometimes she would ask me, "Where are your parents?" Then she saw their condition, unable to see that drinking was causing a ruckus in my family history.

Somewhere in my life I was drawn into the school life. It was a private Catholic school and everyone liked me. Those teachers made sure I had food to eat, had changing clothes, and went on school trips. Time and years went by. When I look backward, it was divine intervention. When I look back, that neighborhood was considered a red zone. It was known for letting loose and use. I was thirteen years old and was drawn into the power of the street life. An experience that had traps and dungeons where people were called nightwalkers. Thanks, it was a time to get loose morals. Traps and dungeons that led to the voiceless pits of hell, and it was where others took control of your journey. The nights on the streets was known for the unknowns, their subjects and their circumstances and substance abuse. That lifestyle was a time spent inside a viewer's hell. You had to get help to escape from it. It was a narrow escape from the toils of a lifestyle of street abuse.

If I looked backward, I was sneaking out of my house at the young age of six. I would leave out of my bedroom window and go to the store late at night. My parents were in a state of too much homemade brew. I was six years old when I took the time to know street life. Drinking and gambling and the late night houses filled with people playing "spades." Spades was a card game that would keep you up for hours, and drinking alcohol, beer and sex was a part of it. We were indoors and not bothering anyone, but the dark forces of hell was making us reach for anything we thought was fun and a unprescribed pill called "microdot" was handed to me. My neighborhood had countrysides, private lives, and hidden secrets which had allowed loose living. Because no one wanted any trouble with police officers, so the mouth was shut. Well, at the time I didn't think it was a negative thing.

Where I lived, the police called it the red zone. A red zone was a place only noteworthy for high crimes. It was my hometown and I thought it was a wonderful place to be and have fun. I was sneaking out my bedroom window at night my parents were asleep. My brothers were younger, but when they were able to walk, they would join me in the street and we headed to the store with the money I saw hanging out of my father's pocket. My father and mother left money loosely around me. It was very dark walking the streets at midnight. Drunks and addicts knew me and my parents. There wasn't known people in my day who would attempt to harm me or my brothers. My father was the neighborhood fortune teller and no one wanted anything to happen to them or their families. So they would just live with their own troubles and leave me alone. My father was well sort out for giving readings to people and he was able to see things happening beforehand. He had a long family history of telling fortune, witchcraft, etc. Some people were afraid of me. They told me that they saw spirits all around me. I thought they were crazy and I ignored them.

There was a lady who had owned that store. Her name was "Miss Sis." She never asked, "Why are you out so late at night?" Her store was the place people hung out. She never told my parents, and eventually I joined the slipping-out-at-night kids. I was the only girl and my father taught me everything I needed to know even when I shouldn't have known. So I didn't want to leave this earth without helping someone get through those situations and circumstances of wanting to be able to be clean and sober. I needed to at least tell someone about my lifestyle experiences and how I made it through. I wanted those awkward things and awful experiences of my life out of me. I just wanted to try and help someone else escape their journey from hell and its abuses.

My Walk
Prayer
God

"Do you love Me? Then feed My sheep" (John 21:17). He is not offering us a choice of how we can serve him. He is asking for absolute loyalty to his commission, a faithfulness to what we discern when we are in the closest possible fellowship with God. If you have received a ministry from the Lord Jesus, you will know that the need is not the same as the call—the need is the opportunity to exercise the call. The call is to be faithful to the ministry you received when you were in true fellowship with him. This does not imply that there is a whole series of differing ministries marked out for you. It does mean that you must be sensitive to what God has called you to do, and this may some-times require ignoring demands for service in other areas.

What has been helpful was the feedback I got from family members, friends, and social media. I was sent text messages that these snippets of inspirational messages were helpful. So many people were enjoying what was being revealed in these messages. As they were reading, encouragement filled their mind and then they were called out supernaturally to become a positive being. These divine inspirational messages gave them a sense of God was indeed confirming and speaking to them about living a better life on earth. The response from so many people has given me the inspiration to put this book together.

Impressions of Love

Let go and let God renew you!

Now it's a new day to receive messages from the Spirit of the Lord…

God hasn't abandoned YOU…

Perhaps you are experiencing a deep emotional, psychological, physical pain from those that didn't love you the way you were meant to be loved! From that hurt, your body and mind took on the toll of inward injuries and abuse! Now is the time for you to be all you can BE. Perhaps you are seeking serious supportive advice. Perhaps this is the day, the moment you will attend and be willing to change. It's time to have a real mental time-out. Take on the signs and supernatural wonders of God to help you grow and develop! The Spirit of God is reaching out to you! CHANGE IS KNOCKING AT your present life!

Push into your destiny.

Get one word from life today that will push you to that new place in spirit, soul, and body!

An Encounter with God

(Updated on July 15, 2014)

> *Enjoy the journey of* experiencing *God's love.*
> *Enjoy the journey* with a different perspective.
> *The journey* living with Holy Spirit leading your plans…
> *Enjoy the journey* that includes the amen (so be it). Try it!
> *Enjoy the journey* with those who are God minded.

April 27, 2015

The Spirit of the Lord says, "With me and my ability, you will not break down, fall apart, neither will you self-destruct. With me, says God, even that which is received will not be wasted or neglected. With me, says God, you will be energized and motivated from beginning to end, completing every project. You will be fruitful and multiply and replenish the earth. You will pursue and recover everything valuable. You will face those impossibilities. Holy Spirit is residing with you, working those things out for your good, giving you that expected outcome. Follow my plans and move into a place of abundance. You are my workmanship, created in Christ Jesus to bring forth good works. I have prepared this in advance for you!"

Take a break right here. Listen to this song "Great Things" by Preashea Hilliard.

October 25, 2015

The Spirit of the Lord says, "Arise, shine, for my light has come directly to you. My greatness is unsearchable. My mighty acts unexplainable, yet I have chosen to reveal to you my ways. The earth shall yield my increase because of what I am calling you to do. I have chosen this day to show you who I am and all the ends of the earth and the foundations of the earth will know that I am your God who has chosen to give you favor. My grace I will manifest on your behalf so you can be effective. Yes, I have shaken the prisons doors."

Immediately there will be an announcement. The Lord of the harvest has arrived to show his mighty wonders. The Most High God is in your very space.

December 22, 2015

The Spirit of the Lord says, "This is your jubilee, a time I have declared favor upon you. Whatever you put your hands to you will receive noticeable favor...my favor. I have proclaimed this upcoming year as a year of God's favor, a time to comfort those who mourn in Zion, a time to enjoy the products of your conse-crating, a time of holy liberty throughout the land, a time of return-ing, releasing, restoring of ownership and rights, a time to get rid of disparity, and a time to receive that renewed hope, vision, and commitment, a time to get that fresh start again, a time of getting rest while being restored. I am the God who has proclaimed that this is your jubilee, the year of my favor" (Luke 4:18).

Experience the beauty of knowing the Creator of heaven.

Being without God is like being without a belt or buckle and you need one. Your journey of fashion and beauty can be smoother having God in your life. The pressure of success can be less intense knowing God as your lover. You can go all over the world knowing that God is with you and will never leave you. You will experience that forever love with God. How can that happen? Believe that God is there for you. It's by faith that you will experience God. He is near you now. He is like the air. He is Spirit. You cannot see him, but he is ever present to comfort your thoughts. He connects with your inner being. He connects with your conscience. He gives you love when you need it and before you need it. He is with you now, waiting for you to allow him to embrace you.

A journey nevertheless.

This new *journey and experience of being in love with God* can take you on a lifelong journey of peace—peace knowing that he can clear your thoughts of despair. He will love you through the hurts and pains of life, the one giving you thoughts of comfort. The only reward of love is knowing God's love is forever. No matter what's happening, he will forgive you. God's love takes you on a forever *journey*. That journey is love especially for you. His love *has* the *capacity to change* you *for greatness*. His love takes you to the highest levels of hope that anyone can obtain. You can experience it right where you are. Can you feel his presence? He is calming your mind. His love for you is reaching those parts of you no one can reach. His love reaches those hurting parts of your being. With his encounters you will feel the room of your heart fill up with his presence just for you. Feel him embracing you. That's it. What you are feeling now is a God encounter or manifestation. He is reaching out to comfort you. He is letting you know that he is saving you from that situation. He is letting you know that you are not alone in this.

You were never alone. He is giving you a right now—new future, new plans, renewed hope for life. He is reaching out to you to tell you do not give up. Do not give up on all-powerful God. He has a better plan that no one knows about but you and him. And he is the one changing your circumstances to help you move forward. He is drawing close to you right now to ease those moments in your life that need it. "All things will work together for your good."

And you deserve to enjoy this great adventure of life because of his love. People can help or hinder your journey. Hold on to the love that God has for you. The secret is having an encounter with God and knowing what you are experiencing is only the love that comes from God. That encounter is believed absolutely by faith—believing that he is with you and no one can take that from you. No one can take God's love from you. He will give away his love to you freely. Reach for it right now. Hold on. God will take you into his care! Trust his love for you right where you are. Feel his love. Take a deep breath as he holds you close to him. You can cry and he is the only one that will understand what you went through at the hands of evil. God will turn your pain into joy. Let him hug you again. He will use your arms to hug you. Go ahead. Embrace yourself and feel God embracing you. Remember how the wind touches your face and you cannot see it. That's the way it is with you and God.

I have learned on this journey of life you must be thankful! You have tried to stay on course without his plans for your life. God will supernaturally teach you to stand while you are going through life's many tests, trials, and tribulations. You will get through it by divine knowledge that comes from God. God has a plan for your life and he will turn those bad situations into goodness and your testimony will help you and someone's life. The evidence will be given to your inner space.

God Speaks

January 31, 2016

The Spirit of the Lord says, "What I require might be difficult to bear, but it is not destructive to my purpose in any way. It is always intended to strengthen you. So right now, get out of the boat and walk by faith and not by sight. Faith is your well of fresh water! Your breakthrough from heaven! Your predestined landmark! It is your hidden treasure riches stored in a secret place, hidden and locked away for such times as these. In the middle of these uncertain times, I am telling you about the faith I have given you. Fight the good fight of faith. Proclaim, declare publicly, announce, maintain, let your trumpet blow. It is written, 'The just shall live by faith!'"

Snippet: This is definitely not the best time to call.

March 12, 2016

The Spirit of the Lord says, "In Ezekiel's days I carried him to a valley of bones. I asked Ezekiel, 'Can these bones live?' My glory will fill the temple. I have seen the glory of the latter house and this house will be filled once again with my glory. Although it looks different from the first glory, it will be greater than the glory that filled the temple in Solomon's days. It will be at full measure, says God! My declaration is that the heavens will no longer be brass and with little fruit. The famine and drought will cease at my command. Let's talk of harvest. You could not have done this on your own. I will endow and we will rebuild. I am calling my people back to work. I have shaken the heavens and the earth, giving new life to the lifeless. The seed which I placed in my people was preserved. I am God enthroned with resurrection power! I will declare my glory! My glory gives fresh revelation!"

March 20, 2016, 6:12 a.m.

The Spirit of the Lord says, "Wait and expect my help, says God. Expect increase while I restore that which is decayed. Again, be strong in faith and you will be able to withstand those upcoming enemies. Renew! Like the eagles, you will ascend and not faint!"

March 20, 2016, 6:12 a.m.

The Spirit of the Lord says, "They that wait upon the Lord shall renew their strength. You will regain new strength. That kind of strength that never existed before. My renewable energy comes from a source that is not depleted or never will be depleted. Wait, expecting my help, says God, to change, to alter, and then to revive, to cause, to flourish again. Expect increase while I restore that which is decayed. Again, be strong in faith and you will be able to withstand those upcoming enemies. My renewal of your strength gives victory over issues, making you able to discharge rightful duties. Renewed strength increases vigor of purpose. With that comes eleva-tion. Like the eagles, you will ascend and not faint. I have sus-tained and upheld specifically being clear and detailed, mani-festing myself, invigorating you while confirming your faith. And declaring your affections for me will rise, saith the Lord."

March 27, 2016, 11:00 a.m.
Resurrection Service

The Spirit of the Lord says, "Some of you will have to be examples others learn from! Whom I choose, I send, I sanctify, reward, and employ in great things or in small gestures, mak-ing an impact. I make my appeal to you through unbelievable phenomena and through the significant and insignificant, my will. Let me remind you about a day I had, says God. I was walking through the streets and behind me the crowds surged and I stopped someone, touched the hem of my garment. She was just a woman in the crowd. If I just touch his clothes, I will be healed. Undistracted faith touched me and virtue went from me to the need. Recognize how things may seem insig-nificant but becomes a part of my great plan! If I don't do the works of my Father, don't believe me, says the Lord Jesus, but if I do, though, you do not believe me. Believe the works, my miracles, which is impossible for any deceiver to perform. Let that be evidence that removes doubt that they are the works of God."

May 15, 2016, 7:29 a.m.
House of Refuge

The Spirit of the Lord says, "Hear, O my people. Many have given reference to the importance of time. Most affectionately I am restoring your time and the years that were stolen from you and satisfying your desires with good things. I am giving back to you a span of time, kronos time, a sacred season of time. Convert it into value. Redeem those moments that really matter. Paul was in prison when I gave him time to handwrite a letter and time for those letters to be hand-delivered. And in one night King Nebuchadnezzar had a disturbing dream and no one could tell him its meaning, but I gave Daniel time to interpret it, and Daniel's career changed for the better! One day, I extended Boaz time, Ruth entered a field, and the harvesters were harvesting and their lives changed and a new destiny started! Transition yourself. Push gracefully into this next season. Hear my voice, my Spirit. Don't be afraid of change. Know that I have altered it. Be encouraged. Press onward to what lies ahead! Discern that it is I who has ushered you into a new time and season, says God!"

Winter has spoken!

The last leaf hanging!

June 12, 2016, 4:00 a.m.

The Spirit of God says, "Help is on its way! If you would just hold on, help is on the way. I am sending those that are able to help others, those that I have approved and appointed. I have arranged the parts of the body, everything, according to its purpose just as I wanted it to be, says God! Many parts, but one body. Each part will have equal concerns for each other. Rejoice! Rejoice! This help I am sending is from me, says God, as a reminder to you that I got this!"

Another Encounter on a Saturday Night

As a citizen of earth, we learn that there are many ways we encounter the presence of God. Each encounter, GOOD OR BAD, can be the potential for greatness. It all depends on how we handle each circumstance we go through. Each step in your life charts out your way throughout your journey of life. It's an ongoing experience that was designed by God for your life purpose. That experience must be well thought out with the inner workings of God. He will give you new plans. But you must be ready to hear him through different avenues. It must be followed God's way. God's love for you will be your guide. It's knowing that he has a *vision* for your life. He will lead you and give you more hope. He will give away what others cannot give you. He will have you sense that it's not over. God has the final answer to your life. And it's all good.

Another Episode 3

An encounter with God which is changing your life forever. Your encounters with God started when you accepted God into your life. It's a freebie. God is always ready to have a special moment with you. It's an encounter that only you can experience and tell others if you want to. The choice is yours, but let me tell you, the rewards are great. Without these encounters with God, only you can *fill* in the blank spaces. Without those special moments, that's a feeling of emptiness and an eternal void. Without God, you will feel really lonely, lost, and very distracted. Without God, you will find thoughts of hopelessness. There is *hope in God.* This is your chance to get freedom from those bad thoughts I just mentioned—thoughts like no one cares. God cares. His love for you matters. He sent you a Savior. People don't want you to know that *but* he is a Savior, for everyone who calls on him is saved. *Jesus* is the door. He died so you can have a better life believing in a better way. Open the door by having faith in Jesus. God can give you good thoughts right now. God can give you a future right now. Don't give up on God. *He is using this* opportunity to reach you and your loved ones. There is a *new life waiting for you.* There is love waiting for you right now. By faith, receive God's love for you. Embrace it. Hold on to this new feeling of love. This kind of feeling is renewed every day. Just say, "I love you, Lord God" and watch God love you right back. Feel him comforting you and leading you in the right direction.

Encounters 4

This connection with God can be a lifelong journey. It only ends when you let go. But God will never let go. He will always be there to pick you up after time. And that's okay. He wants you to need him. This life's journey of yours can have bitterness and sweetness. Make your decisions based on the divine Word of God. *Stay awake* while you are on this journey, finding peace and purpose. It's a divine connection purposely made for you by God. He predestined you. You need this connection. *Remember:* everything can *change in one second* for your good. Let God change your journey for the better.

Make that connection with God.

*****

Good morning. The weather outside is cool. It's 7:02 a.m., sunlight blazing the sky. I had a wonderful chance to talk with a friend of twenty-five years. It's a good feeling knowing that God places people in your life. And when you meet them, you don't know how they could ever be lifelong friends. You don't know it but God set you up! God allowed both of your paths to cross and the both of you became a great part of your destiny of healing and long-lasting friendship. Through situations on both sides, your friendship added positive value to your lives. Learning to share your ups and downs with someone is healing. Even thoughts of your whatever life is truly a healing! Stay with it! Because you asked God to grant you *serenity* and he used a great method, tailored, made plans just for you!

The Spirit of the Lord says, "I have gone before you. You will live and not die and declare my signs and wonders. To the one who has, more will be given [Mark 4:25a]. Expect it and receive that undeniable increase you in me and I in you! Whether you are young or old, your fruit is going to grow, *increase*, and remain. What distinguishes the good ground is fruitfulness. Its beginning is small, yet it increases! Let me remind you of my word, says God. I have gone ahead of your circumstances and cleared the pathway. By faith receive more grace, an enlargement in purpose, and grow exceedingly through the power of my Holy Spirit. You are a candle of light. Your *life* will shine and be obvious. You will increase in humility and patience knowing who I am to you. Go ahead and let your gifts be useful. Do not neglect your office. Stir yourself up for my glory."

Cultivate a little solitude.

"Solitude makes us tougher toward ourselves and tenderer toward others; in both ways it improves our character," noted philosopher Friedrich Wilhelm Nietzsche. Spend some time away from the crowd and the noise of life. Set aside a few minutes to be alone—just you and God. In quietness we turn our minds away from the problems of life and fix our thoughts on the mind of God.

Worshipping God

Occupy till he comes.
Read Luke 19:12–13:

> And said unto him, occupy; negotiate, or
> trade, that is, with the pounds; make use of
> the ministerial gifts, exercise them, lay them
> out, and trade with them: the ministry is a
> trade and merchandise, to be carried on, not
> in the name of the ministers of Christ, nor
> on their own stock, nor for themselves, but
> for Christ, and for the good of souls; which
> shows, that they must not be slothful, but
> laborious and diligent: till I come: which sug-
> gests the certainty of Christ's coming, the
> continuance of the Gospel ministry to that
> time; and that there is no rest nor ease for
> Christ's ministers, but a continued series
> of labour and service, until then; when, for
> their encouragement, they shall receive their
> reward.

The Vision

Though it tarries, wait for it (Habakkuk 2:3).

The Spirit of the Lord says, "We cannot bring the vision to fulfillment through our own efforts but must live under God's influence and inspiration until each step is fully fulfilled."

Example: Is it a good idea to charge into a battlefield unprepared?

At the beginning, God gives you a vision. If you proceed through without the guidance of Holy Spirit, you are rushing off and forward without divine directives. Waiting for that inward peace, unction, confirmation, divine guidance is a true testimony of our faithfulness in God! We must wait until God selects the spot.

The Spirit of the Lord says, "Don't let this life talk you out of what I have for your end. Your history is not over... Better times are ahead. I have not given you an empty way of life nor any empty dreams. I am not a God who flatters and I am never at an uncertainty. I have promised only the best for you. I alone know your final purpose and my purpose for you will be made known in a manner that cannot be denied. I am consistent and unchangeable. I am moving about designing and settling issues. Jeremiah 29:11 is true. You have an expected end, a very desirable one, such as you are hoping to have. I have given you my written word, a promissory note. Though it tarries it will be an expected end, the enjoyment of good things.

Yes, those things you have been waiting to see, to hear, and to touch!"

The Spirit of the Lord says, "I know, says God, that at eighty Joshua and Caleb led a generation of young people through a desert to a promised land. Two old people who had to face overwhelming circumstances and tough choices but with renewed faith, hope, and dreams had to press onward. It meant 'straining their faith to new limits.' Crossing over into new territory meant trusting me. And by faith they took me at my word and I went ahead of them, clearing pathways. And no one was able to stand against their faith. I am declaring in your hearing, says the Lord of host, 'your strength will equal your days' [Deuteronomy 33:25b]. For I am stirring within you renewed strength. That effort and ability to go forward, to flourish, to grow and bring forth fruit in old age, and to enjoy the fruits of your labor. Those fruits which are beneficial, which are appropriate, and then leading you to be my divine course of action, for these things are a gift from me. Do not think much about the fleeting days of life because I will keep you preoccupied with my peace and joy that which derives from my presence and my activity."

The Spirit of the Lord says, "What I require might be difficult to bear, but it is not destructive to my purpose in any way. It is always intended to strengthen you. So right now, get out of the boat and walk by faith and not by sight. Faith is your well of fresh water! Your breakthrough from heaven! Your predestined landmark! It is your hidden treasure riches stored in a secret place, hidden and locked away for such times as these. In the middle of these uncertain times I am telling you about the faith I have given you. Fight the good fight of faith, proclaim, declare publicly, announce, maintain, let your trumpet blow. It is written, 'The just shall live by faith!'"

The Spirit of the Lord says, "Excel in strength. For my eyes, says the Lord, run to and fro throughout the whole earth, to shew myself strong in the behalf of them whose heart is perfect toward me. Your eyes have not seen nor your ear heard, neither have entered into the heart of man the things which I have prepared for those who love me. I will make you ruler over many."

Ride Those Waves

The Spirit of the Lord says, "Go ahead, ride those waves. I am holding you up! Don't let go. It's written in Psalms 107:24–30, a mighty wind blew and the waves stirred. The ships were lifted high in the air and plunged down into the depths. The sailor's courage diminished. They stumbled and staggered like drunks and their skills were useless, but in their troubles, they called out to me and I saved them from their distress and calmed the raging storm, and the waves became quiet, and I brought them, says God, to the port they wanted. You will be okay because I have a grip on you. It was a narrow escape because of the pressure of issues and responsibilities. You didn't know you could be a surfer riding those waves steady. Hold your hands up high. Surf those waves of adversity for I am Jehovah Shammah, there with you, an experienced surfer."

The Spirit of the Lord says, "Know my depth. A controversy was going on among twelve tribesmen as to who should be performing which tasks. Each tribesmen was given instructions to bring a tribal rod representative of their tribe. Moses took the twelve rods and placed them in a sacred place. I was the one who testified that day, says God, the workings of my incredible depths and distinguishing something specific and remarkable. Only one rod stood out among the others it budded, blossomed, and brought forth almonds. Aaron's rod. I will testify again, creating marvels such as the world has never known and no nation has ever experienced. I am a God of

Truth whose will is to distinguish you from all the others in the earth."

The Spirit of the Lord says, "You must perceive that you please me, says God. Pleasing me involves you obeying the work I have called you to do. Your faith and desire to serve me pleases me. Continue stirring yourself up, strengthen those within and round about you! And be strong in my grace. Do you know I was there when my beloved Peter tremendously blew it? says Jesus. He denied me three times. But his faith was evident that he wanted to please me."

What's wrong now? Ah, cheer up...

The Spirit of the Lord says, "I am Jesus, the mediator of the new covenant. Again I have shaken the heavens and the earth in order that the things that cannot be shaken may remain. Arise for I have changed the course of events. Once again my consuming fire has gone ahead of you, using power to change those circumstances and giving due victories. I am going to fulfill what I have promised and my list is endless. I am also stirring up the Spirit of the revivalist and bringing a due season of open doors forward. Make this your Instagram moment as I bring in the fulfillment of those hidden dreams and long-forgotten visions. Believe this: if you can see, it is nearer than you secretly thought. Check my text messages, says God, I left words of encouragement."

The Spirit of the Lord says, "Get ready! Joy and laughter will return and fill your heart. You will see me fill my sanctuary and validate my name. Be astonished. Your plans will be established, says God. I am unshakable, unwavering, and impossible to change, and truly committed to keeping my promises. My loyalty is to fulfill my obligations. You are hemmed in by my love. What I have promised I will confirm with miracles, signs, and wonders. What I have written shall come to pass. Hear and acknowledge my might. I told Abram to open his eyes, look around, look as far as he could see in every direction. Enlarge your vision. See greater things. See your victory and success. See the increase of your children. See the salvation and glory of the Lord. Open your eyes and see my abiding presence!"

The Spirit of the Lord says, "I am giving you a new level of courage. I am intentionally taking you to greater heights in me. Ask me what I am doing. And I will tell you! For I am the Lord of Host who can disannul it. My hand is stretched out. Who shall turn it back? I am bringing you through this same bothersome situation, giving you a new level of courage and confidence. It is my desire to manifest my presence while you are even now in this fiery furnace. I am the one who has prepared you and allowed those fiery trials to come and go. You are more than a conqueror. My very presence is going through this and going through that with you, giving you a new level of courage, turning situations around so you can continue to bring me glory, honor, and praise. You are like a tree that is planted by water. Don't fear. Continue bringing forth precious fruit. A new level of courage is taking you from faith to faith and glory to glory. Like an eagle, keep a steady focus, yes, a mental note card, while Holy Spirit show you he is your Representative."

The Spirit of the Lord says, "Arise, the fog has lifted! On the way to Canaan, a land of promise, Jacob wrestled a divine wrestling match. You are at that place wrestling your divine wrestling match and you are wrestling by faith! Your wrestling has established a double portion, says the Spirit of the Lord. Your portion is twice as much, beyond the normal measure, sufficient, and impartial! It's that abundantly above all you. Ask or think impartation of power and blessings simply stated a wrestling match of believing faith is bringing your breakthrough!"

The Spirit of the Lord says, "The oil of Holy Spirit trickling downward, precious and highly valued oil, prepared for you before the foundation of the world, breathing a breath of fresh air without and within. I arousing the divine within and around about you. My sound and my wind is reaching your forgotten depths, causing transformation and new beginnings. I am repositioning the church for power, spiritual alignment, divine unnatural occurrences. Hear me, says God. I am declaring and decreeing the cancellation of negative assignments and dismantling the works of evil destruction. I am releasing divine wisdom and authority in many places: I am releasing revelation, discernment, and unwavering support."

The Spirit of the Lord says, "Observe closely a paradigm of words and actions. Can you put new ideas into old mindsets? Can you get new results with old behaviors? A fresh pliable mind can absorb expansion and slowly age with a fermentation process that I complete, says God. An old idea can assume a definite shape but can no longer be pliable. It is fixed and somewhat brittle. The activity of a renewed mind will put stress on an old idea and pressure it beyond its ability to yield. A renewed mind has a definite inspired shape. It is a time to be pliable, a time of reflection, a time to take stock, to evaluate, and a time to position your strength in the land to embrace new directions. Make it not a classic New Year's act. Undergo a fundamental change in one's mind/character. Simply put grace is the voice that calls one to change and then gives the power to pull it off. Do not be afraid. Do not be discouraged, says God. Before I formed you in the womb I knew you. Before you were born I set you apart and consecrated you. You are a fertile land well able to produce fruit."

The Spirit of the Lord says, "It can be of great encouragement to be aware that I am the only God that remembers, listens, and hears. It is written in Genesis chapter 8 that I remembered Noah on the ark 150 days and accomplishing what I intended for his life and the lives of all my people. I remembered Hannah and Rachel and gave them a child. I am letting it be known that I do hear my people and answering them, letting others know that my will is being done in the earth. What I am doing is being recorded. Do you remember what happened to Paul and Silas in jail at midnight? What about when Sarah laughed within herself? I heard her and confronted her. Do you recall what happened next? I have a scroll of remembrance written in my presence concerning those who honor my name and reverence me. I will not forget their labors of love. I will spare them. Nothing in all creation is hidden from my sight, says God. Everything is uncovered and laid before me. The cries of my people reach me and I have seen the way many are oppressing them and I know what is done and who I am sending to get it done. Awareness is all about me and the needs of my people are not forgotten. Believe this above all other things, that I am a God that remains trustworthy."

The Spirit of the Lord says, "I am a God at hand and not far off. My words give power to feed the soul. I speak knowing the end from the beginning and all things are always before me. I told Abram to open his eyes, look around, look as far as he could see in every direction. Open your eyes, give it all you got. Stay focused on what I have given you to do. Let your eyes look directly forward and keep that gaze toward that vision for it ascribes from me. It is my revelation and ordination. You have been sat apart to see and to hear, having prophetic insight. I have shown you what is and what is to be. Continue working with commitment. Let those plans be established. Let it not be a castaway or be hijacked. Fuel prices go up and so it is with faith. Make your faith clear, having no remorse or regrets, says God!"

The Spirit of the Lord says, "What I require might be difficult to bear, but it is not destructive to my purpose in any way. It is always intended to strengthen you. So right now, get out of the boat and walk by faith and not by sight. Faith is your well of fresh water! Your breakthrough from heaven! Your predestined landmark! It is your hidden treasure riches stored in a secret place, hidden and locked away for such times as these. In the middle of these uncertain times I am telling you about the faith I have given you. Fight the good fight of faith, proclaim declare publicly, announce, maintain. Let your trumpet blow. It is written, 'The just shall live by faith!'"

The Spirit of the Lord says, "I have not gone out of business. Nor have I given the silent treatment. I see tomorrow more clearly and the future is completely in my hands. A new day will dawn. And my unfailing love will not be shaken. I have outlasted every question and remain skilled in all endeavors, ever watching over everything and knowing what is best. Lean not on your own understanding, but in all your ways acknowledge me and I will forever direct your path. You will always be a well-watered garden, completely satisfied even in a sun-scorched environment. This is what I do, says the Spirit of Truth."

The Spirit of the Lord says, "Consider this: Prepare to use uncommon faith. Prepare the way for the oil of Holy Spirit to trickle downward. These are uncertain times calling forth very precious and highly valued oil of Holy Spirit. You have been prepared to have mountaintop experiences where God himself will speak directly, manifest, and change your name and life."

Spirit of the Lord says, "So get rid of that uneasy feeling because I am releasing throughout the land and to my chosen ones prudence, a practical application to increase in making inventions. I am awakening the spirit of those that are equipped to use their craftsmanship. It is a time for witty inventions. I am giving you the ability to produce new results, well-considered, carefully thought out designs, plans, conclusions. For these challenging times, says God, I am giving you bright ideas. Crisis is really your opportunity in disguise to use wisdom. When a famine came, I gave to Joseph divine wisdom and Pharaoh saw something different and promoted him. Daniel developed a healthy diet during a time of significant challenges which brought glory to me, says God, and Pharaoh saw something unique and was compelled to promote Daniel! It is your time to develop those crafty solutions, clever devices, and increase in innovations! I am giving you an opportunity to reinvent, redesign technology, and come up with new products and procedures. This will enhance your life and you will produce better solutions where others lack vision. With a vision such as witty inventions and new ideas, society improves and learns new ways of doing things! Right now I am increasing your capacity for creative thinking… Receive."

The main reason a ship needs to launch *out*!

The Spirit of the Lord says, "You thought it was over. Launch out! Every dream that's in your heart, and every promise that has taken root, I put them there, says God. I have power to induce labor and require new things to come forward. Just because it has taken such a long time to manifest and because you've tried and it seems as if you were failing doesn't mean that your dreams aren't going to happen. In Luke 5:1–6, Simon had been fishing all night and caught nothing, but I told him to launch out into the deep and let down your nets for a catch. Simon said to me, 'Nevertheless at your word' and he launched out again and caught fish. Don't be complacent about pursuing what I have placed in your heart. I am who I say I am. And it is written in Isaiah 45:3, 'I will go before you and will level the mountains, I will break down gates of bronze and cut through bars of iron. I will give you hidden treasures, riches stored in secret places, so that you may know that I am the LORD, the God of Israel, who summons you by name.' I am the only one who will make a way out of no way and make sure every promise is fulfilled."

The Spirit of the Lord says, "The main reason a ship needs an anchor is to ride out storms so that it is not blown off course or into the rocks or reefs nearby. I want you to get this understanding what I did at creation. I have given you a safe harbor and an anchor so you won't drift, hit something, and sink. Maybe you didn't understand what I did. When I spoke at creation, the event took place. The animals came forward but with you I created, formed, and fashioned you with my hands and filled you with my mysteries, signs, and wonders. I made you in my image, blew my breath into you, and gave you my Holy Spirit. You are my blessing, says God, my appointed vessel, my workmanship, and I count on you being anchored in me doing great things until the end comes."

The Spirit of the Lord says, "I am merciful when you are not aware that I am helping you get through those issues, circumstances, and situations. My grace and mercy is that something that gives evidence of my divine favor. Grasp that significance. In a world of constant changes, it is easy to feel overwhelmed, to be facing something that you have never seen before. I will show you the surpassing riches of my grace and mercy in those crucial times. Grace and mercy is not merely a part of the plan of redemption, but it is the silver cord that runs through every facet of your journey of life. It is the established work of redemption. When all else is said and done, every element of my work, says God, will be revealed throughout and you will experience personally my daily output of sufficient grace and mercy."

The Spirit of the Lord says, "I am more than a watchman. At the end of my watch I hold myself accountable and know when to intervene and deliver my promises. I have a covenant responsibility to be a careful watchman and know when there is a need to sound an alarm to warn my people of impending danger. This is my now word, watch as Holy Spirit carefully perform those visions of things to come and bring you more opportunities to work in my vineyard. I am watching you come out of captivity. I am reminding you that I am a careful watcher and sounding an alarm that your waiting period has apparently come to an end. I have intervened on purpose and those promises I clarified are on course. Press on…for I am restoring your cheerful outlook and watching you come through the gates safely. No matter what it looks like, I am giving you my peace. Holy Spirit knows those unseen predicaments, problems, or difficulties that can overwhelm you. Rest knowing when it seems to be absolutely no solution in sight, I have provided that solution and will make a way out of no way for you. And at the end of my watch, you will have my reassurance that I am who I say I am."

So it was a starry night sky and I took one of those trance-like glances forward. As I looked straight up and into the night, there was inside of me words from my inner being which spoke, "How naive can ones thoughts be."

The Spirit of the Lord says, "It's a new day. This is my position within and throughout life: revitalization and recovery. I am giving you renewed health and well-being. I am that lifelong… livestream of Zoe life—the life of God that assures abundance of life that overflows into success and richness. I am using you to recover and restore my kingdom attributes. Reviving the spirit of the lowly and brokenhearted. I have given them a spiritual hunger for more opportunities to experience things of the kingdom of God on earth as it is in heaven, things that will bring back the meaning: you are alive! Remember: I have placed greater things within your heart and those things you long for will come to pass. It is written in Matthew 5:6 "Blessed are those who hunger and thirst for righteousness. For they shall be filled."

The Spirit of the Lord says, "In Acts 27:13–14, a nor'easter had sieged Paul's ship and the south wind blew fiercely. The wind was howling and the waves pounding and seemingly no signs of help. There was a change at once in the force and the direction of the wind. The crew aboard ship was so close to their destination, very close to their delivery point, when the storm burst upon them. And Paul had perceived and gave them a grand example using spiritual essentials a calm trust in me, says God. And he rendered that cheerful encouragement to those on the ship during the storm. The crew was doubtful of their journey, thought of their troubles, food scarce, and impossibilities prevalent and their danger of sinking. But Paul, whatever his position, kept hope. Timidity and fear was infectious, and his cheery voice had revived those drooping spirits. Paul spoke, giving them wisdom and good reason. It was because Paul owned that he belonged to me, says God, and that he served me, and that anything was possible with God. He believed and spoke from faith rather than that I would leave him unhelped at such an hour of need. He believed in me, says God, and that I would give evidence of a journey through according to my divine planning. I am who I am. So arise. Be of good cheer, and in due time the event will warrant your faith in me and my promises even though all around seems to make your faith folly and your hope a mockery."

The Spirit of the Lord says, "Get out of that cave. In biblical times David was pursued by King Saul and continually escaped him by hiding among the rocks and caves. Those circumstances made David thrive, blossom, succeed, advance, prosper in the midst of his transitioning. David was weary during those years of flight from Saul. Each transition was seasonal in David's life before he became king. Those storms in your life was not the destination but the pathway to your destination. It meant you're being prepared for something. Make a visual note. It is impossible to get from where you are now to where you are going without making several transitions. I have strategically positioned you, says the Spirit of the Lord, so you will be able to access things you could not access beforehand. So come out from those caverns, move forward staring destiny in the eyes."

The Spirit of the Lord says, "No matter what it looks like, you are resilient! Able to rise up and make a difference. In the face of those challenges, those stones will move out of your way and you will have a positive outcome. Believe that I can do something at any moment that could change the direction of your life, says God. Believe you are more than able to recover and spring back into shape quickly. You will rise up and be that something new that never existed before. It is written in Isaiah 40:29 that I am He who gives power to the faint, and to him who has no might I increase strength. I have given you that peculiar ability, that bounce back and you will succeed. I am working with you with signs and wonders following. I am confident that you will rise up and complete this new journey, says God!"

The Spirit of the Lord says, "When you see who I am, the only appropriate response is one of humility, says God. Ezekiel recognized the difference between us. Ezekiel understood his place and the appropriate posture he should take. In humility, he fell facedown before me. It was in this posture of humility that Ezekiel heard from me. He experienced the presence of my glory. When I saw [it], I spoke to him and told him to get up from that posture. I watched as he responded in action to my requirements."

Though it tarries, wait for it. (Habakkuk 2:3)

The Spirit of the Lord says, "We cannot bring the vision to fulfillment through our own efforts but must live under God's influence and inspiration until each step is fully fulfilled."

Example: Is it a good idea to charge into a battlefield unprepared?

At the beginning God gives you a vision. If you proceed through without the guidance of Holy Spirit, you are rushing off and forward without divine directives. Waiting for that inward peace, unction, confirmation, divine guidance is a true testimony of our faithfulness in God! We must wait until God selects the spot.

We are not empty or alone in this but have Holy Spirit within us!

The Spirit of the Lord says, "Be still and know that I am your God. From the pulpit to the courtyards you took a risk and have proclaimed the biblical good news. I know you have gone through challenges, opportunities, cycles of days, months, and years. I want you to look at your reflection of me in you. See me in you. See my glory shining on you and reflecting off you. In Isaiah 60:2, it is written, 'The Lord will arise upon you, and his glory will be seen upon you.' I have put my glory on display for you. Don't get it twisted. I will demonstrate my qualifications to you and for you. I will announce to the world that I am your God and you are truly my people. I will move heaven and earth to bring you your breakthrough! I am really who I say I am. I am Lord of the Sabbath."

The Spirit of the Lord says, "I am Lord thy God who has seen your tears and all your tears are recorded. Each tear is counted for your consolation. Even I, Jesus, wept tears of compassion and ultimately eased deep sorrows and sent immediate comfort and restoration. I am well able to comfort your soul and spirit, giving refreshment of mind and spirit. Through it all I am he who will come alongside of you offering my assistance, counsel, and exhortation. Indeed, I have come alongside you, and through it all I will keep bringing you that unexplainable joy. Where else can you expect it! I am Father of mercies, God of all comfort, who knows how to comfort you my people! I heard God and he spoke and said my people are speaking what I want to hear and those that don't believe will see my hands move throughout the land. The weather and situations are truly a testimony that I will reveal myself and will answer my people. There is a need for me to bring back the peace my people need so much. I can do it and will do it, says God. Many will turn to me because my people are declaring their love for me and I am declaring it to them. This is my opportunity to show that I am on the throne."

The Spirit of the Lord says, "You must perceive that you please me, says God. Pleasing me involves you obeying the work I have called you to do. Your faith and desire to serve me pleases me. Continue stirring yourself up, strengthen those within and round about you! And be strong in my grace. Do you know I was there when my beloved Peter tremendously blew it? says Jesus. He denied me three times. But his faith was evident that he wanted to please me."

The Spirit of the Lord says, "Don't give up! Pursue. Recover all!"

The Spirit of the Lord says, "To the one who has, more will be given [Mark 4:25a]. Expect it and receive that undeniable increase!" Whether you are young or old, your fruit is going to *increase*. What distinguishes the good ground is fruitfulness. Its beginning is small, yet it increases! Let me remind you of my words, says God. You will receive more grace, an enlargement in faith, and will continue to grow exceedingly through the power of Holy Spirit. You are my candle of light. Your *life* will shine and be obvious. You will increase in humility and patience and use your gifts for public usefulness and not neglect them but will stir them up for my glory. Wherever I send you there will be an incredible increase of favor. Wait and watch in due time. You will be discovered!"

The Spirit of the Lord says, "When you see who I am, the only appropriate response is one of humility, says God. Ezekiel recognized the difference between us. Ezekiel understood his place and the appropriate posture he should take. In humility, he fell facedown before me. It was in this posture of humility that Ezekiel heard from me. He experienced the presence of my glory. When I saw [it], I spoke to him and told him to get up from that posture. I watched as he responded in action to my requirements, and I will bless you in everything that you put your hands to. I am extending unmerited favor reassuring you that I have not left you alone but is opening up supernatural opportunities."

The Spirit of the Lord says, "And let us not be weary in well doing, for in due season we shall reap, if we faint not" (Galatians 6:9). Then God said, "You can search all over and you will find nobody greater than me, so don't be discouraged, fatigued, or fearful for in due time you will receive in your lifetime an abundance of sustenance. Yes, that healing sustenance which gives support, endurance, and strength. I will not withdraw but will send nourishment to keep you alive and active. I will send you an outlet of nourishment that's actively sustainable. Do not grow weary in well doing. Your seeds shall spring up and gush forth to overflowing and you will see and enjoy the fruits of your labor. It is my will that you be blessed. And I have intentionally, deliberately, purposely, knowingly blessed you above all that you have asked for or that you have even thought about, says the Most High God."

The Spirit of the Lord says, "Increase. What distinguishes the good ground is fruitfulness, its beginning is small, yet it increases! Let me remind you: you will increase! Wherever I send you there will be an incredible increase of favor. Wait and watch in due time. You will be discovered! Shout out loud for all to hear in the sanctuary. I will be there for you and your family, and your life will always have the presence of my glory."

The Spirit of the Lord says, "It has been a cycle of days, months, and years of opportunities and moments of doing what's divinely right. It is certainly interesting to know on one day, there was a commotion in the courtyard and Jesus was being led away by soldiers. A betrayal had been made. Judas Iscariot had sold Jesus for thirty pieces of silver. Judas literally left his ministry of serving me, says God, to serving under the influence of evil, that popular secular perspective. I am requesting divine dedication with eternal life ramifications. I have called you to be a representative of a great mission and have placed something incredible within you and in your life! I have placed an emphasis on you to choosing this day whom you will serve. And making right choices is a divine discipline and your personal breakthrough. So you won't be perfect at this age, or any age. But you'll be *ready*! Ready for whatever I have in store for your life."

The Spirit of the Lord says, "Aaron's rod budded, blossomed and brought forth fruit. I am giving you a greater measure of my blessings. My desire is that my glory come on you in a measure greater than you have ever experienced and can be seen upon you and your loved ones! When you experience my glory you will experience more of my favor, healing, protection, and supply than you have ever experienced before. My presence is being manifested. My glory has taken up residence and there are no barriers. You were specifically designed to bring forth greater works of Jesus Christ. I have sent you. Make no mistake about it. It is I, Jehovah Shammah, who is dwelling in your mist."

Jesus replied, "Go tell that fox that I will keep on casting out demons and healing people today and tomorrow; and the third day I will accomplish my purpose. Yes, today, tomorrow, and the next day I must proceed on my way. For it wouldn't do for a prophet of God to be killed except in Jerusalem!" (Luke 13:32)

The Spirit of the Lord says, "There are moments a teacher is silent, no longer instructs, but let that person showcase those skills which they have learned. I am a great Teachers, says Lord Jesus, and I am silent during the test period. I have entrusted you with a greater purpose. Not only I am silent, says God, but silence brings about value. Job went through my silence and several different things happened. It was a divine setup. After all his questioning and struggles, I spoke to Job in a voice from out of that storm. I asked Job, 'Where were you when I began the work of creation?' Job knew that my silence never equaled my inactivity or absence or purposes. I am consistently working behind the scenes for your good and my glory. When it seems like I am not doing anything in your life, stay very close to me, says God, and watch. I will display my power and affirm something great for you and for those involved in your life!"

The Spirit of the Lord says, "For to the one who has, more will be given [Mark 4:25a]. Expect it and receive that undeniable increase! Whether you are young or old, your fruit is going to *increase*. What distinguishes the good ground is fruitfulness. Its beginning is small, yet it increases! Let me remind you of my words, says God. You will receive more grace, an enlargement in faith, and will continue to grow exceedingly through the power of Holy Spirit. You are my candle of light. Your *life* will shine and be obvious. You will increase in humility and patience and use your gifts for public usefulness and not neglect them but will stir them up for my glory. Wherever I send you there will be an incredible increase of favor. Wait and watch. In due time you will be discovered!

The Spirit of the Lord says, "The times and seasons are not under the control of chance. I have ordered the events, says God. In Psalms 37:23, the steps of a good man are ordered by the Lord, and he delights in his ways. Ordered: given an authoritative direction and instructions. Each of your steps I have directed and placed them. So you are where I meant for you to be. I have given inspiration to those steps and strategically ordered and established your destiny, making certain each step is on purpose. You being present in a situation is enough to influence that situation. I am the one who has allowed the times and seasons in your life to stay on course and to complete the necessary processes. Time goes by, I will connect each event in your lifetime to your purpose. Every experience you have experienced, without a doubt, will help to establish my divine purpose for you, says Lord Jesus."

The Spirit of the Lord says, "Do not despise my great work. For I rejoice to see the work. My eyes search all around the world, not by human power but by the aid of my providence and grace, with Holy Spirit's oil pouring in secret and in an invisible manner, without the help of man. My Spirit pouring and causing someone to take action, causing someone to be triumphant over all opposition. Observe further in ancient times and even now I speak to people's hearts, causing them to build. My work, says God, is often carried on very successfully and earned on very silently, without the assistance of human force, not by might or power but by my Spirit and through the Spirit pulling down strongholds successfully. Take note that the excellency of power is of God and not of man. For I will not forsake the work of my own hands, says God."

The Spirit of the Lord says, "Holy Spirit is working his power in your day without that divine power leading and guiding you. You will be just spiritually lifeless, just another somebody. Without my holy power helping you do the work, that inspiring work will not get done. I have placed something good within your spirit so those assignments can have a final outcome. Expect Holy Spirit to lead you completely. Don't hide that God-given ability to conquer! Through it all, arise, being watchful. Launch out again and listen intently to my directions. Focus only on those tasks that I have set before you. And at the end of my appointed time, those tasks will bring victory to you and your family, says God."

The Spirit of the Lord says, "I know you're counting on me, says God, and I will not let you be disappointed. I keep my promises. At my word things produce and fulfill all of my purposes for which I send it [Isaiah 55:11]. So when you hear the word, even when you are sleeping and ignoring it, my word takes on my ways and the process is etched in life. It works regardless of whatever is going on. What I promised you is working out for you. It is working now on your behalf. It is working in a way that is invisible to your eyes. It is working on that situation you keep thinking about, the one you're praying so earnestly about. Here's my secret, says God. My secret is in the seed, not in the soil nor in the weather nor in the cultivating. My word is the seed which I have placed before you, and it is working according to its own natural design. Its growth is a mystery. Though it tarries, it will without no doubt be found faithful. Though it grows invisible to the natural environment, you will witness that my words are eternal, alive, and active."

The Spirit of the Lord says, "Do not despise the work I have called you to do for I rejoice to see you working in my vineyard. My eyes search all around the world, not by human power but by the aid of my providence and grace searching for the one who wanted to know and serve me. Holy Spirit's oil pouring now in secret and in an invisible manner, without the help of man. My Spirit is pouring into your life and causing you or to take action, causing some to be triumphant over all opposition. Observe my ways, and in ancient times, even now I speak to people's hearts, causing them to plant and build. My work, says God, is carried on very successfully and carried on very silently, without the assistance of human force, not by might nor by power, but by my Spirit and through the Spirit pulling down strongholds. Text this message that the excellency of power is of God, and not of man. For I will not forsake the work of my own hands, says God.

"I am leading you right now!

"Think and believe what I am promising you, says God. I am working all things out for you. It is working now on your behalf. It is working in a way that is invisible to your eyes. It is working on that situation you keep thinking about, the one you're praying so earnestly about. The same one you have been holding inside."

The Spirit of the Lord says, "I have given a description to those that are in Christ. They are genuinely a new creation. A new conversion lives within them and they are filled with a new perspective. They move on into the future by faith. They move toward those things that bring them a greater purpose! A new course of life is truly living within them. A new attitude emerges from them and expected Holy Spirit is actively involved in their lives, causing all things in their lives to work together for good, especially for those who love God and are the called according to his purpose. It is an effectual call. God said, 'I have designed it to be so and isn't that so amazingly peculiar that I have given them faith as a covenant door that brings in the newness of life and divine favor. This observation is as important as it came.' I have bestowed my honor on the lives of those who believe! And they will walk in my ways, declaring that I am truly working things out for the good of all involved!"

The Spirit of the Lord says, "I am stirring you up and stirring people up to help you get the work done. The Lord said he is doing it!"

God is giving the reader enthusiasm, active interests, and passion for their goals or assignments. So everything you need can get done!

> Then Haggai, the Lord's messenger, gave this message of the Lord to the people: "I am with you," declares the Lord. So the Lord stirred up the spirit of Zerubbabel son of Shealtiel, governor of Judah, and the spirit of Joshua son of Jozadak, the high priest, and the spirit of the whole remnant of the people. They came and began to work on the house of the Lord Almighty, their God. (Haggai 1:13–14 NIV)

The Spirit of the Lord says, "I know you're counting on me, says God, and I will not let you be disappointed. I keep my promises. At my word things produce and fulfill all of my purposes for which I send it" (Isaiah 55:11).

Store this in your life:
So when you hear the words of encouragement, even when you are sleeping and ignoring it, my words says God will take

on my ways and the process will be etched into your life. It will work regardless of whatever is going on.

The Spirit of the Lord says, "You can search all over the world and find nothing no greater than reaping my great rewards. For it is written in Galatians 6:9: 'And let us not be weary in well doing: for in due season we shall reap, if we faint not.' Don't be discouraged, for your time and season is expected to come. I am a Sovereign God who has established plans to make sure you receive that needed strength. Receive and expect the unexpected outlet of nourishment, unimaginable opportunities, life-changing miracles filled with joy unspeakable which I have commended you. I am sending you strength for the journey. Let it spring up and gush forth to overflowing."

Thus saith the Lord Jesus: For a servant is worthy of wages. (1 Timothy 5:18b)

The Spirit of the Lord says, "Death and life are in the power of the tongue, and those who love it will eat its fruits" (Proverbs 18:21). "Your tongue is a great weapon for good or evil. Take the consequence of your words. Fill your mouth with life, not death. An unexpected word of kindness can change a life, says God. Did you not know that tongues include hands that write, type, paint, or sign? The tongue can be "a tree of life." It can reconcile people. It can make peace or war. It can spellbind a nation. When you, my people, speak your character passes into action. By your words your own immortal future is affected. Put a watch on your words, exercise life-changing influences. Know the power of your words which are infinitely reproductive for good or bad. This is the stuff you should remember, says God!"

Really…appreciate your new journey of life!

Push into Your Destiny

The Spirit of the Lord says, "One day I got into one of the disciples' boat on Lake Gennesaret. The one that belonged to Simon. Peter and I asked him to push out a little into deep water and lower his net for a catch. He told me that he had been out there all day and didn't catch any fish [Luke 5:4]. At that point Simon needed his faith to take the place of sight. He needed to trust what I was telling him to do. Directed service. His choice in that moment was a pivotal point of his destiny which would have affected the rest of his life."

The Spirit of the Lord says, "You're going somewhere. Push into deep water, push into that unfamiliar territory, push into new depths, and let down your nets for a catch."

The Spirit of the Lord says, "I am the Lord your God who has seen all of your tears, and all of your tears are recorded. Each tear is counted for your consolation. Even I, Jesus, wept and my tears of compassion is extended to you. I have ultimately concluded, I will ease your deep sorrows and send immediate comfort and restoration."

My
Passing Through
Fulfillment and Contentment

Personal Messages
Inspired by God

Stories and Encounters

Believe

Before Manifestations

Believe what God's Word says about you. Have you experienced secret encouragement from God to go onward and open
up to others by sharing your testimony? Did you know that the
rewards are felt on both sides? Those who have shared their
testimonies of how God intervened in situations has been helpful. Only God could have come to their aid and handled their
personal predicament.

Know that God is changing things. Declare and decree that all
things in your life be placed right now in order and that negative
things be considered null and void. Speak now of faith to that
situation, that it has no authority over God's intense plan to give
you and your friends and families abundant life on earth as it is in
heaven. Command divine blessings to come forward. Command
the heavens to open and send forth divine directions from the
north, south, east, and west of this land and that the angels of
the Lord's armies do battle to bring about heavenly provision to
you in Jesus Christ's name. Declare that Jesus shed blood rest
and rules; always abiding with your life and command your body
to be healed and to get in line with God's Word. Amen!

It starts with having a positive teachable *spirit*.

Sharing snippets of your life and inspirational moments will change your hurtful memories. Get your life back and *hope* in God!

> "In the same way I will not cause pain
> without allowing something new
> to be born," says the Lord.
> "If I cause you the pain,
> I will not stop you from giving birth to
> your new nation," says your God.
> —Isaiah 66:9 (NCV)

I Am a Prophetess

This is what God has revealed: the authority and nature of the gift of prophecy is to prophesy.

Matthew 10:41 is receiving a prophetic reward. The prophet's reward is the fulfillment of the prophesied word and this reward requires effort to receive. This is where people so often miss the fulfillment of the prophesied word. It's not a matter of making it happen; it's a matter of cooperating with God by faith.

Remember, in ancient Greece, episkopos, "bishop," could refer to any official who had a supervisory function, an ordained, consecrated, or appointed member of the Christian clergy who is generally entrusted with a position of authority and oversight. To do this job well, an episkopos had to be intimately aware of what people were doing. He had to watch out for them to ensure they were prepared for anything that came their way.

Christ, the incarnate God himself, is the holy loving bishop of our souls. He is concerned for us and looks after us to preserve our souls and empower us to fulfill his purposes for us. Just as our Father in heaven knows every hair on our head (Matthew 10:30), so too does the Son has his eye on us every second. Indeed, he is concerned with even the smallest details of our lives. "For the Lord sees not as man sees: man looks on the outward appearance, but the Lord looks at the heart" (1 Samuel 16:7).

The prophet's reward is the fulfillment of the prophetic word. There are two ways to receive a prophet's reward. The first way is to do what the prophet does: trust and obey. The second is to receive a prophet as a prophet, which means that even though you haven't heard the Word from God for yourself, you trust and obey the word of the prophet to the point that you act on it by faith. This is a fact for God has given humanity free will, and as such every one of us is free to accept or reject the prophetic Word of God. However, while we do have this freedom, it must be acknowledged that with every exercise of our free will, every decision and every action we take, there is a consequence in the spiritual realm which alters the material world. Prophets represents God. They go forth from the presence of God and speak what God has given them to speak. The prophet speaks the Word of God in the power of the Holy Spirit. It is not just speaking the Word; it is speaking it forth in the power of an anointing borne out of intimacy with Jesus himself. The prophet is the ambassador of Christ in this world, and so the prophet and his message are inextricably linked. A true prophet cannot be separated from the message they bring. Neither can the true prophet be separated from God. When God sends someone to speak forth his Word, then he/she is speaking it on God's behalf. Rejection of the prophet and his message, therefore, is rejection of God and his Word.

> He who receives you receives me, and He
> who receives Me receives Him who sent Me.
> (Matthew 10:40)

Because the Word of God is alive and active (Hebrews 4:12), when it is received, it takes root to bring forth life, just like a little seed.

> And whoever will not receive you nor hear
> your words, when you depart from that house
> or city, shake off the dust from your feet.
> Assuredly I say to you, it will be more tolerable for the land of Sodom and Gomorrah
> in the day of judgment than for that city!
> (Matthew 10:14–15)

You see, if God wants to speak something to you and me, then he wants us to have ears to hear it. There is always a purpose to God speaking, and that is to bring forth life. To close our hearts and our ears to him is actually an act of disobedience. Remember Saul. He shut his ears to God's instructions and, because of his disobedience, was rejected as king. I feel that there are some in the body of Christ who have rejected a Word from the Lord because it didn't sit well with their flesh. Perhaps it seemed too big, perhaps they felt inadequate to receive it.

My Personal
Encounters

I Am Tired of Seeking My Parents' Approval. I Am an Adult

Why do you always think it's me causing the problems? You never think it's you. Mom! Dad! Why do you think it's never you causing the problems between us? This situation between us has been going on for years. So I messed up. Both of you are still holding this issue over my head.

I am tired of seeking your approval.
I am an adult.
I got to go!

Before we can deal with our own afflictions, we must recognize that they have a divine purpose in our lives. Each situation we go through helps us to comfort those that go through the same situation. It gives us a chance to teem something from the adversity. It gives us a chance to really love people for who they are. It gives us a chance to be humble. "Many are the afflictions of the righteous, but the Lord delivers him out of them all" (Psalms 34:19 KJV). We have a divine promise that God will deliver us out of all of our afflictions.

Deliverance. Everyone's deliverance is different. It could start with just saying something or doing something to make the situation better for you and your family. It's about keeping the love you have for one another as a family. Okay, so what if you are always the one that keeps the family together? It means you have strength of character. It's okay as long as peace and love is restored. It means you are able to work situations out to glorify God.

Love has specific characteristics, especially when you have to put forth effort. It's called a demonstration without conditions. If you are the one that reaches out to keep the peace in your family—good. You'll feel better. You'll feel better knowing you tried.

Another point: call a family meeting.

Keep notes.
Let everyone speak to clear the air. Pray first that everyone will come to the meeting to resolve issues. Everyone should come up with a plan on how they would like the issues resolved. May the best plan be voted on by the majority rule ethics (old or young voting).

Honor your father and mother.
There is a blessing that comes with it. You get healed! You get healed knowing that you put forth the effort to respect and honor your parents. And it releases you from a whole lot of mess. Get freed up. Make up your mind to forgive your parents. Do it in person and live! Kids (old or young) have to be taught good family values. Why? So they can keep them up even into adulthood.

Are you listening to your adult children?
But God gives us a tender way on how to handle each matter. One matter at a time.

You Cheat! You Thought It Was a *Secret*

I hope you didn't do it... You know!

If you did, I forgive you!
Designed for truth. Secret things come out in the open anyway.
So you thought no one would find out... Okay.
I just felt something different about our relationship. Honey, will you explain why you are doing things differently?

We have been together for quite some time. I sense something. Intuition is telling me that there is someone else. Why aren't you talking to me? Honey, I noticed some things left in your car that calls for explanations. Why can't I look at your e-mail? Why did you close your computer when I walked in the room? The telephone has been ringing and the caller hangs up. Oh, I forgot to tell you I had the number traced. Why are you so quiet? Honey, my friends said something to me that seemed very strange to me the other day. Your car was parked... Mom, what's that odd smell round about you?

My heart says you cheated on me. But inside of me, deep within, I am hoping you did not cheat. I have come to believe that every hidden thing comes out. Yes, through time it is revealed. I know I had a part in this. Perhaps I stopped growing to be the best I could be. But excuses still do not allow you to take advances beyond our commitment. Now what are we to do with our relationship? Trust has become the issue. And with that, other issues have sprung up. Are you going to secretly do it again? Do you have a problem with keeping a one-on-one commitment? Wait a minute, until we decide it will not work, should I still love you knowing you violated our harmony? The truth of the matter is...can you face this reality that you have been accused of cheating? It's not about me. It's about your integrity to face what happened. All this tells me is that you gave me an indication that you are not telling the truth. What gave it away? Was it the way you were treating me? Honestly, I do not want to talk about this again. Honey, do you hear me? (No response.) Honey, honey. Wait, if you did it, I forgive you. Honey, wait!

Wow, I wonder why he left me.

No Money to Bury My Loved One

So this is what I did…

(Updated on June 17, 2013.)

The purpose of this is to tell you about my experience during a hard time in my life and saving money. One year ago. August 2008. My husband died and panic came to my mind. Well, you got to plan ahead and keep going. You have to go to plan F. (A, B, C, D, E worked and now there is plan F.)

F is when everything else fails and you start making things to sell. Everyone's plan F is different. I was thinking how could I save money and pay bills. Being creative… Great idea! So start making, baking, and creating things to sell. Selling slices of cake to family is one of my ideas.

When times are hard, you tend to get creative.
When you need money, the mind can get creative.

Buying apples and turning them into candy apples. Nice idea, right? Selling candy apples and ice cream to working family members. Family is your first store buyers. They seem very happy to invest in family success and creative adventure. It's only an idea during hard times.

Family will show up and be supportive. They will show up and ready to pay for the homemade everything. Homemade hamburgers will work. It works. The hamburgers seasoned. They will love it. Homemade pizza is a must.

I am still generous at times. But...times have changed. Coupons too. I saw this lady with a grocery cart filled with food. The food in her cart looked like it would cost her $300 dollars. But by the time she got through the line, it was $46 dollars. She had coupons.

So what if your family talks about you? When you live in an apartment building and the people think you are so friendly and nice, they come to your place for eggs, small items like milk, vitamins, makeup, soap, soda, extra that or this until they get paid. Leave a donation please. I am not playing. Times are not the way they used to be. It was about plan F. Also, creating games and making money.

Okay, back to the real reason I wrote this hub.

My husband passed away (died, August 2008). Well, the funeral home wanted to charge me X amount of dollars. Way too much money!

My pastor said, "Can't you order wholesale online?" We checked online and I saved over 5,000 dollars (buying funeral supplies, casket, etc.).

That's why I am sharing this good news with you.

Order online.
Have the shippers ship items to the funeral home. There is no law that says you cannot save money. I had to save money. I ordered everything online and had it shipped to the funeral home. I saved myself and my family over 5,000 dollars doing it that way. Everything went well. Some places charge too much during economic hard times. So I had to, in the midst of my sorrow, learn how to save money. Burying a loved one is hard and even harder when you got X amount of money.

My husband passed away unexpectedly. I had to wake up and think how was I going to bury him when we just cashed in the insurance policy two months before he died. We went on vacation and had a good time. After twenty years of marriage, we needed a shebang and we did it up. Listen, it's time to tell. Times are not like the old days. The days when you just had the extra money. It's time to save and be creative, especially when you drive a Mercedes! *And people think you got it.* Let me continue.

So his body was in another state. And he had to be flown back to the state we lived in. The funeral director said he needed to come back in a special refrigerator. The cost for a special refrigerator he had to be placed in, etc., the cost was beyond thoughts. I said special refrigerators for shipping dead loved ones. I hope this doesn't happen to you but I was saving money. Let the truth be told.

Escape

Go. Do not look back. Reposition. Go. It's not over until it's over and you are free. You can escape from that hell-raising relationship. Your situation is only a good start to freedom!

Through the mountains.
Through the mountains.

Go. The situation seems... Let your survival skills kick in. *Do not look at how hard* the situation seems to let your survive. *Refocus. It's not over until* it's *over* and you are free...

Keep it simple:
ESCAPE.
Get a tent.
Use night-vision binoculars.
Get a backpack.
Make it PERSONAL.

You can escape from that hell-raising relationship. Your situation may seem like there is no hope for a better life, but that's not true. Let me take you through this journey of escaping the hell you're in. Let's begin by going through tough survival training skills. The first skill is walking by faith. With God you can do all things because his words will strengthen you to move forward. Take that faith; walk through those rough places in your life. It may seem like mountains of problems with no solutions, but there is a way of escape. Start thinking. Some people fail to start thinking of a way out. They focus on the problem. Take a deep breath. Tell a reliable person to help you think; two heads better than one. The plan is to tell people so if anything happens they will not get away with it, etc. Tell...tell... Expose the enemy by telling. Make it known that at times give that person a wake-up call. YOU MUST DO SOMETHING. THAT'S WHERE YOU start. I am telling this as you make your way out. You must get through that mountain of fear and doubt. Go...

The journey through the mountains can be rough, but if you plan you can and will survive that experience. You are scared but you must press. It's your journey and you will see your way out. There are people waiting to help, whether you are male or female. I know men go through abuse too. For many reasons people have a hard time believing that people do abuse people and they put on a front. The abuser will put on a front in front of others, pretending that they are nice. You know they are not. Get over it and get your life back. They are abusers and people get abused. And it is possible for you to be a victim. But if you are a male reading this, get your freedom so you can be a helper to someone else in trouble. More abused people that we can help; at least one more person will help end this abusive sickness by exposing it. It's about freedom and helping those who are held captive against their own will. Cultural or religious freedom is the way. I believe a person should feel free to choose whatever they want and not be held against their decisions. You should be as free as the wind. Lay out your strategy and go forward.

NOW FAITH.
Use your plan

The day I decided to leave and had everything planned, I was cooking dinner. He did not like what I cooked, then he went to the stove, took the food, and threw/slung the food on the floor. I had planned to fight my way out. I picked up the hot water and food and went at it. I had a lot of stuff lined up for battle, etc.

TEN YEARS of abuse. I was hurt, young, scarred, but I had decided to go forward. That day I was going to get out. That day I had four pots on the stove, hot and boiling. I was tired of getting beat up: punched and kicked and there was more sex after being beat up. I felt like…you fill in the blank. So that day I fought like hell. I threw pots, etc., fighting like it was the last day on earth. The hot food burned him. He went to the hospital and he said that when he gets back he was going to kill me. He left and I waited, and minutes later I took off into the dark. I was scared. CRYING. I did not take clothes because everything looked as if I was coming back. I went underground. I had planned ahead to seek shelter. There are shelters out there in the world that will hide you and your family. But you have to say, "This is the day I am going through that mountain." You can get money by asking for small change from fifty people and hide it. A bus ticket or cab is still cheap enough to take you to another state and get into an emergency shelter. When you get there, go to local police; they have a list. Make it a start for a new life. You may have to move again, but make up your mind to run like it's your last day. Don't tell people your plans because it will get back to the abuser. GET OUT!

I lived through it to help you. YOU have to want to live free too. When hope is removed from a person, they quickly deteriorate and begin to die. Never give up your HOPE. FREEDOM IS KNOCKING AT YOUR HEART. Go "take the WIND OF CHANGE."

When you are getting ready to make that move, start telling the most important people. On my job, I told the security guard because they would be on the lookout to give me a signal if they saw my abuser. Next, the shelter was aware before that. Then underground I went. I went into hiding. You must have plans. WHEN IT'S TIME TO GO, MAKE UP YOUR MIND AND JUST GO UNDERGROUND (another state).

READ THIS TO MOTIVATE YOU.

When you are in trouble, there are fifty (50) ways to leave and get out, fifty ways to the north, fifty ways south, fifty ways east, and fifty ways west.

FIFTY WAYS TO THE RIGHT.
AND FIFTY WAYS TO THE LEFT.
AND RIGHT DOWN THE MIDDLE.

Find fifty reliable people that can and will help you. Give fifty reliable people a sign that you are in trouble. Tell them of the abuse. Let fifty reliable people know that someone is taking advance liberties that you do not want or like. Give fifty people a secret sign that you need help—a code, etc. The reason you need fifty reliable people is because one person is not enough when you are in danger. They might not get the help you need. Fifty reliable people will give you more hope of getting the help needed.

Your freedom and happiness is important for you and your loved ones. Don't be afraid to tell the news media. The more you expose it, the better of a chance you will have to survive this bondage. Do not sit there and do nothing. Stay alert because the person that is harming you does not know everything. There is a way out. Find your way out. You must see the way out. Your abuser is so busy watching you. But the secret is you are looking the other way to get out. I believe you will be free to move around. Find the door out of that place. I had to make up my mind that day and I left. I made up my mind to fight for my right to live without someone controlling me. Stop destroying yourself. And stop letting others destroy you. Get free help. It is available because so many people have escaped. It does not matter how important they are. You have a right to your life.

Men face bondage as well. A whole nation of men could be living in fear, afraid to voice one thought of freedom. They throw truth out in order "to live." For the men in this situation, you can get free too. Just get the help you need. Finally, let these words encourage you to get the help you need. You need these words to motivate you to go. Remember that isolation is the abuser's key. UNLOCK THAT DOOR NOW! Tell...tell...tell and go forward to get your freedom. THINK OF FIFTY PEOPLE THAT CAN AND WILL help you. No excuse. TAKE A DEEP BREATH. One hundred reliable people = 1 dollar each = 100 dollars. Get to a shelter in another state. Get your plans together. Remember: YOU TALK IT OUT. THINK IT OUT. WRITE IT OUT. PLAN IT OUT. Just get out. MAKE SURE IT IS A PLAN THAT IS WELL THOUGHT ABOUT. And that is simple. YOU WANT OUT. Just remember to complete the journey TO GET OUT, WALK IT OUT, WAIT IT OUT, RIDE OUT, HIDE OUT.

It's YOUR JOURNEY. And it must be and CAN BE A SECRET. KNOW YOUR PLAN. REMEMBER: FIFTY PLANS AND FIFTY WAYS.

Find who you are. You do have a future. You are someone special. And you can help someone else get free. It can be a journey, just long enough for you to feel the breeze again on your face. Long enough to dream again, hope again, and find a new life. It's your *time*. GET away. Your *journey* is your journey. There is shelter everywhere outside of where you are. Get your freedom back. Think about it no longer. This is your chance to escape that unhealthy relationship. THIS MISSION IS NOT IMPOSSIBLE. The only way out is to get out of that unhealthy environment and relationship. WHEN YOU GET out and there in that safe place, that place where you are going, grab hold of your inner peace—the peace you had longed for. My advice: run like hell is coming after you. Run and hide. Run and hide. HIDE until you feel you are no longer under that unhealthy experience and relationship. Keep God in your heart!

This is a thought provoking message to you, the reader: How do you want your journey of life to end?

Save Me, Lord God

God heard you. He is God and has power to save. He knows your inability to save yourself. Yes, you. I know you thought you just stop to read. But God has a plan to save you supernaturally. He drew you to a place where He wanted to tell you that saving you is His original plan. Stop what you're doing and just think about it. Some people will come to this site because of this system where you write a hub and people are notified. But it was different for you. God drew you to this site by his Spirit. Salvation is your gift today. God has a special purpose for your life. He knew at this time you needed to free up your thoughts and let God reach you. You might even say today, "I'll talk to God about my situation. If I get an answer I will live again. I will hope again." Well, you have come to this site by God's grace. You did not have to do anything to get God's free gift of salvation. God sent Jesus to save you. It is by faith. We receive God's plan of salvation through the sacrifice of Jesus's life by faith. We may have missed it with God and done things that do not please him. So we ask him to forgive us because we have done things that wasn't pleasing to God. So God's plan is to reach out to everyone. And he is reaching out to you. God is reachable. He is reaching out to give you needed victories over this life, giving you the ability to function in this life. Cry out, "Save me, Lord God."

Next: we must admit that we missed it. Believe that this snippet was God's plan to save you. His power raised Jesus from the dead. Resurrection power. God will use that same power to raise you up from dead works, visions, and dreams. That same power will cause you to change your old life for a better one.

Next step: confess now, followed by faith that God set you up and is your Savior. He can save you from any situation because he is a deliverer of all things. That same God that made this great universe is the same God that is saving you right now. Make it personal. "Save me, Lord. Save me from destruction." God is using this event to help you get another grip on life. God is reaching out to you. The Almighty God has become your Father, your Hope, your Peace, your Anchor in times of great need, your Savior in the middle of a crisis. So go ahead and make your confession.

"God, I know this is you saving me. I believe it by faith. I am receiving your saving power right now. I have made a wonderful decision to make that confession right now. Only you know my secret place. I truly confess! I am saved."

So if anyone asks you, "Are you saved?" your answer will be or has changed to "God saved me while I was doing me." Remember, from this day forward, you belong to God's family. You are his child. By faith in God you are saved, for everyone who calls on the name of the Lord Jesus is saved. Salvation is received by faith. Faith is trusting that it is so without seeing it. Everyone who knows God knows how to get us back on the right path. God has called us to turn our life around and live. You have a purpose, a God-given purpose. God stopped you, right where you were, to tell you that you were created to do great things. Some people look too far. But that great thing may be just offering your service (small or great). You were made to make a difference in this lifetime. Find something to do and make a difference. Just smile. Offer a thank you or give someone a cold glass of milk. Tell yourself, "I can do something good for someone!" See results every second that you're a new person with a new journey because God remembered you and saved you from self-destruction.

Can Looking at Your Face Cause You to Change?

Your face can be a good *reason to change*. Does your face tell your life story? Your face can show problems or tragic moments that came across your life. This can be an opportunity for God to use someone to encourage, to comfort, to exhort you to complete the journey to change your outlook on life. Your face and body can be a reason for change. The fact is you have to face your outlook on life. When you face that inner you, things about you begin to change you. And that face is what people see when they meet you for the first time. Here is your opportunity to change how people look at you. I know you thought I was talking about your natural face, and I am. But I realized change begins from within. This is an opportunity for God to use you by changing how you think about you. God changes a person from the inside out. It is up to you to reach into your heart and want that change. God will reveal to you many reasons for change. Here are some examples: if you talk too loud, lower your voice. Are you willing to take suggestions and change you? It's about making you better and letting your facial expressions show it.

Your face is what people see when they come into your personal space. Are you willing to go the extra step to change your facial expressions that lead to the inward you? That means finding ways to change. Then taking the next step and follow through. Changing your face starts by doing what is needed. That's what it takes to change that behavior or lifestyle: changing by doing. In order to change, you must put in that needed effort to change. It takes effort on your part. The wisdom will come to change, but you have to do your part. Change the way people perceive who you are or what you will become. When you become aware of your face, it will give you the ability to move forward and to know that change is needed—either from destructive patterns of behavior or nondestructive lifestyles.

Changes on your face causes changes to your outlook on a lot of things. Your face is what people see when they get close to you personally. Your ability to change can become a reality. People will notice something new about you. Are you willing to go through training? Are you willing to submit to changing your face or body? It takes effort on your part. Start with a simple change. Start with looking at you.

That ability to change can be as easy as thinking of other ways of improving your self-image. That is the mystery for you. You need to improve on your self-image. You need to motivate yourself. Tell yourself that you are going to finally love you. Love yourself enough to want to improve your self-image. Take heed. Start right here, where you are, knowing you need a new journey. Move ahead and change. Get a glimpse of what God is trying to say to you. Know that it is God who is truly trying to hold you up. Just remember this scriptural verse: "But with god all things are possible." Don't debate about it. Facts are facts and you can change your outlook. God has the power to help you change.

When you believe in God, that power is available. That power that comes from God can be just what you need to move forward in life. You will not know it until you receive it. Use faith. Faith is believing before you see it. God's power can change you from the inside out. You can become that new creature in Christ Jesus. His power will free you from your past. God's power will give you a new hope for a new life—a life you have never seen before. Remember: it starts from the inside out. Your facial expressions will begin to describe it! You are different and people will look at you differently. You will see yourself change for the better. You will have that new identity given to you by God. You will become new all over. God will give you that new self-esteem and then that new image.

Say "NO FEAR from my inside to my outside. I am changing and my face is showing that change." You will be supported by God's encouragement. This access is gained by faith. He will send you the power to experience your change. Exercise that authority to change. You do that using affirmations. Exercise that authority to change you inwardly to outwardly. Make the decision. Decide that today is your day to get ahead. *Decide* now that it's your time to change your facial expressions to positive expressions. Don't look back. *You* must decide to change and start being all over positive. Believe what God says about your life through his Word. You are his beloved. You are truly amazing and more than a conqueror through Christ Jesus. Every person has a different journey custom-made for them. Each person needs encouragement to make that difference. Here is one secret: it's a mystery journey through life and with God, he turns bad things around for His good. *Wonderful changes* come about when bad things happen. A chance to make a bad decision or situation change for the better future. It's a chance to improve your life and the life of those around you.

Question: Does your face tell your life's story?

Get Away from Bad Habits

Breaking That Opposition

Bad habits can be linked to having a bad inner spirit—a bad inner spirit that can cause you to have or cause you to have malicious desires that can spring up from within you. Those malicious desires can take over your thoughts when you are not in control of your actions. Those malicious desires will plague your soul then move through you and your purpose of life, *and people think you got it*. Bad habits that can at times dominate through the power of suggestions.

Repeated negative suggestions. Those negative suggestions may produce negative behaviors. Those negative behaviors have a tendency to make others put you outside the norm. Those bad habits may cause you to repeat unacceptable society acts over and over again, consciously and unconsciously, to the point where you can become unaware that it's a bad unacceptable habit. God's plan is to get you to start functioning according to acceptable living standards. Being aware of bad habits is the first key. People will notice your bad habits before you will. When you become aware that you have a bad habit, hopefully you will listen and correct that situation.

Unlearn bad habits and learn good habits. Everything we do is a learning process. Be willing to get outside help. Be willing to change that behavior.

Get help.

Bad habits that do not fit in with society norms may cause a person to do things to others that are not acceptable in society. People just think these habits make them feel uncomfortable. The problem is that, bad habits, if you do have them may cause harm to yourself and others. Responding to bad habits may cause you to have an internal war because you don't like your bad habit.

You may start to have prolonged struggles in other areas of life. Prolonged agony, meaning inner struggles, conscious or unconscious, and your thoughts get worn down and you begin thinking, "IT'S CALLING ME!" the urges get stronger and stronger until you tell your brain, "*I feel the need...*" "*I cannot help it...*" "*I need it!*"

In other words, the thoughts to commit the act becomes over-powering. The thought to commit the act gets so intense to the point of committing the act. My personal suggestion to you is to get a substitute in its place. You need a power that exceeds that desire just as great to overcome that bad habit.

To me a bad habit can be abandoned by following God's plans; think on getting another one, a better way to help you change. A bad habit can be a strong *force* that takes your thoughts captive. Money to get drugs. Doing anything to get drugs (selling your clothes, children, etc.). On your mind is etched doing drugs or that bad habit. All it takes is a moment and a strong powerful destructive thought to force you to do that bad thing.

Strong powerful destructive force or thought that comes to your mind and that thought or suggestion makes your character respond correctly or incorrectly. And then you fall prey to it, good or bad. You have to get tired of being driven by it. Afterward you will feel better or worse than before. You have to put your mind on letting it go. Committing the act places you in a temporary state of unawareness as you snap out of the trance that you did not know you were in. It's not until you did the bad habit that you become aware of the hold it has on your being. Get help.

SNIPPETS

Bad habits can be broken. That bad habit can submit to God's divine authority. You have to be personally persistent and fight back the thoughts, things that hold you back from going forward with your life.

Fight back the thoughts for your thoughts, a conscious battle that only God can help you with.

Stay away from people, places, things that trigger the habit. Remember: it's a mental fight to stay clear of the habits. It's a "fighting the enemy" decision. It's listening to the *voice* of God whispering to your heart! Keep quiet and listen to that *still small voice* of God. By faith, *listen...*

Personal Testimony

When I was faced with my habit, I was with the person that triggered my habit. I was sweating and thinking no, no, no. The moment was intense. There was a distraction that helped me greatly. I was at my weakest point and I stayed focused. I won that time. You will always be faced with the habit. What you learn is how not to fall prey to it.

Simple! Sometimes we look at Or for the big answers and it's the simple facts that helps. *Simple*! The Bible scriptures help us, giving us encouragement. It is written that: "*The battle is not ours but God's.*" God can help us, deliver us, just with his words of hope. Read the words of God and be renewed in the spirit of your mind. JUST HIS WORDS OF HOPE can make you feel better. Sometimes we live looking in the wrong direction for answers. The answers are found here inside the Bible. The Bible has been a great help to people for many centuries. If you give God's word of knowledge a chance, it will change your life forever. The delivering power of God's Word has the power to change you and your circumstances. The delivering power of God's Word of knowledge will help you break bad habits. Reading the Bible can help you to change the way you want to do things. It will encourage you to break those bad habits, overcome addictions, conquer self-destructive behaviors by seeking God's plan.

God will always send support. He will send people on your path on purpose to enhance you with encouragement. He will send people on your path to pray for you, to comfort you and motivate you as you go through your life. God has definitely designed your destiny. Your destiny is designed by God and he will turn things around for your good. A well thought-out destiny ordained and protected by God's love for you.

This will be the *best love affair* you will ever experience. *Knowing* that God will be there for you is the best gift you can have. This will make you happy! You are a child of God. Your life without doubt will change. You can count on it! Feel God's blessings for you. Feel God empowering you to complete the divine tasks set before you. *Complete life*. He will reach out to you right now and you embrace it. Feel that divine encounter. Move forward knowing that a better future is ahead with God being always with you.

With God in your life and spirit, you will grow in knowledge. With God all things are possible. Experience and embrace the things of God. Draw close to him in prayer. Seek his rewards and pursue a better future. He gives those who believe; receive that long sort out peace. He can bring your *dreams* to pass and give you a feeling that you will *accomplish* every task. God's love will give you that peace knowing that he will work your future out just for you. He will give you what you need when you need it. Only God's love can save you at this moment. Trust me, I have been there. I needed his love. When I needed his love, he drew close. As he is drawing closer to you right now, God will stir up the power to have joy. Obtain from God the ability to hope and dream again. Let God reconstruct your destiny so you can win. You *choose*. God gives you the opportunity to choose. He lets you decide if you want his help. You know you need God's plan. You need his help and comfort. When life seems impossible, reach for God's love. You need that God kind of love. Let his love fill your life. Let him reach your inner soul and give you that peace and healing balm. Let God's encouragement bring you opportunities to move forward with joy. He will give you the ability to continue on your life's purpose. God is the life coach that will always be your valuable gift. He will give you strength of character and spiritual boldness.

*****

Throughout my life's journey I have learned the power of God's love. He will draw you by his mighty signs and wonders! He will manifest himself in His very essence. You and god become one spirit. You will want all that he has for you. Read Jeremiah chapter 29 verse 11. no greater love have I found like this. No one can be in your spirit like God. Passion at its ultimate level… Spirit to spirit, his presence will scoop you up and place you on solid ground.

*****

I am hoping you accept God. He will hold you close. He will protect your interest and give you a safe place to sob, to wonder, to dream, to hope. He will tell you that you are his.

*****

He will tell you about yourself and that you're the future. You will experience recovery when it's in his timing.

If you feel ALONE OR LOST within A GROUP, in the mist of all that, God will be there for you. *He will never leave you nor forsake you. Accept his love and be everything you were meant to be. Others will be drawn to your story because of him.*

You will find the joy you need, the *success* you want, the *love* encounter you hoped for *(literally and spiritually), and your destiny* will be secured.

I loved him no matter what. What is *love*? This information in this is relevant content to those that can love others no matter what. They can say or tell someone that they love them because they are lovers of life, liberty, and of people. I *love you* even when I…

See

See Your Promised Land

See, this book was designed to briefly explain the need to see faith as having spiritual eyes—eyes that can see beyond situations and circumstances. The eyes of faith releases power to emerge and to move you forward. Everyone should visualize their strengths and successes. That takes gazing with belief. In the book of Joshua chapter 6 verse 2, God told Joshua to see. God planned for Joshua to conquer the land of Jericho, but he had to see it happening before it did happen. Joshua had to look beyond the normal circumstances and see victory. There were giants on that land, but he had to see himself taking ownership of the land of Jericho. He had to see beyond that six feet thick wall that was also thirty feet high. He had to see beyond that land that was filled with ferocious warriors. Joshua had to take heed to God's command to see.

See your recovery. See better circumstances. See your comeback to victory. See yourself free from whatever is holding you hostage. These brief notes are showing the need for you to look beyond distractions and capture a vision of better things. Joshua had to see beyond what was before him. He had to see a future. He needed to see beyond that wall having no doubt or fear. When you take your eyes off of the darkness of doubt and fear, you will see into a better future. It will take you exerting visual thoughts of that future being better. Use that God-given faith which has eyes to see the blueprint of your life. That kind of faith sees with a clear view.

Believe. God will give you a clear vision of your purpose. He has given you that kind of faith that charts mental pictures, explores, and gives you an experience, helping you grow inwardly. That inward visual experience causes the mind to be stimulated, moving that interest from vision to actuality, therefore changing your performance outcome. After a visual experience like that, people generally consider moving toward that vision in the future. Proceeding with that visual information causes changes that will encourage you to push forward through traditional ideas. You will see more movement from the brain to the next level out of the brain to action. That vision can be hindered known as procrastination.

How can a person thrive to see? Each believer is given an opportunity to see their land of opportunity. That opportunity is to see yourself through the journey of success. But you can fail to look beyond ordinary life. Distractions can definitely be designed to cause a person to abort their vision. Each person must stimulate their mind by using the power of reading. Read about your vision. Note in a journal what you plan to do. It can stimulate the brain back to sending information to the inner mind and to review those plans and press on to carry those plans out to support success. This may not make sense but disappoints can alter your thoughts. Keep a journal. Make predictions of what you think you see happening as you continue to work on changing. Keep journal records; it will help keep you on point. It's a record, a way to read what is seen in the vision, revealed insights. Write down what the brain flashes on it. Write about your vision and its perspective. Read what you wrote and get an understanding about it. Let it stimulate faith and increase your seeing beyond the natural. Let the outcome exceed human expectations.

With God all things are possible when one believes. A person can choose to look beyond the natural issues and visualize better things to come. The power lies in trusting that God has predestined you for better things and you can have that vision. You must be that person who believes that God has the power of turning things around for your good and works those plans and purposes out for his glory. Following that God-given vision will benefit you and others. God planted that vision within you. One must believe that God has power to turn every opportunity around for your good, especially when he has a positive outcome for you and has given you a vision for your journey through life. Here are some important keys: (1) learn to see: practice visualization; (2) speak with God: pray; then (3) conquer with actual action.

In Joshua chapter 6 verse 2 (NIV), it says, "Then the Lord said to Joshua. 'See. I have delivered Jericho into your hands, along with its king and its fighting men." This victory began in a vision. God told Joshua to "see"! Before anything happened, Joshua had to use his inner eyes and see Jericho's wall coming down. That wall naturally was six feet thick and thirty feet high and filled with warrior soldiers and harsh people. Read it and understand what God is saying to you through this brief book. In 2 Chronicles 18:4, Jehoshaphat always said, "First seek the counsel of the Lord!" But during this period, Jehoshaphat did not follow God's plans. God will always give guidance to look beyond circumstances and "see." See beyond the natural circumstances. We are living in uncertain times and it is causing us to see a lot of bad everywhere. But God is calling for believers to see beyond their natural ability. Joseph in the book of Matthew chapter 1 had to face a situation where he had to see and use uncommon faith. The kind of faith that included a vision of the issues of his life, the life of someone else, and what was revealed to him in a dream. He had to exercise faith that was uncertain and uncommon during his time. In Matthew chapter 1 verse 20, this was Joseph's experience quote: "But after he had considered this an angel of the Lord appeared to him in a dream, saying, Joseph, descendant of David, do not be afraid to take Mary as your wife, for the Child who has been conceived in her is of the Holy Spirit" (Amplified Bible). His situation called for Joseph to use uncommon faith by being a visionary and moving forward. God gave him a vision in a dream and placed it into motion for his life and others. Joseph had to visualize what he saw in a dream to see guidelines for his possible future. He had to take heed and respond. He had to use insight. Whether good or bad, the insight was before him. Joseph was given a vision, a dream, then an access to respond. Joseph had an inward knowing. He used that inward knowledge from God, which helped him to see ahead. His response was actually a moving forward by using uncommon insight. Having insight and working with uncommon faith increases the ability to move forward. Uncommon faith means out of the ordinary, unusual, odd, peculiar. He recognized and considered that this is God's plan. Joseph was given the ability to see beyond the ordinary what could have transcribed, and he chose to walk by uncommon faith. It was a time to see the plans God had established. Those plans of God were revealed to him in a dream.

Learn when it is of God, looking or perceiving that it is his doings, then follow that inward knowledge that this is of God and his plan. Joseph still had a choice to be considered to follow the plan that God had placed in a dream and in motion or his own plans. Joseph considered the dream and vision. Considered means (Greek word: "noeo") to perceive with the mind, think about, ponder. And "katanoeo": to perceive clearly, to understand fully. Seeing the vision via insight comes first then accepting it by faith. Seeing with insight is God's purpose. He makes promises beforehand that you will always conquer. He will cause that vision to come to pass. Then take heed and see what God wants you to see. Finally, God has given believers power to see beyond the natural—a plan to see spiritually. Seeing is implying implementation: to look, see, and/or pay attention to the vision with intent and earnest contemplation and following it. The lesson to be learned is to see beyond the ordinary and to be prepared to walk by uncommon faith called insight!

This is not "fake news"and 'It- is -what- it -is.'

The most powerful weapon that defines you is hearing God's voice leaving you with an everlasting impression. It will grab, transport and intrigue you while captivating your thoughts. You will consider reading John chapter 10 verse 27. King James Version, "My sheep hear My voice, and I know them, and they follow me."

Within Snippets you the reader, will be given, no matter where you are, no matter what's your situation an opportunity to be cognizant of God's voice speaking through Snippets. As you read through Snippets God's purpose for you is to give you incentive, a drive to get up and go leading.

About the Author

Dr. Brendell Thomas Francis holds a BA in Psychology, a Masters in Human Resource Counseling, Certified Life Coach. She is the CEO and Founder of Daughters of Tamar and Tamar Community Outreach where she brings women together from all backgrounds of life enhancing their lives by intensifying, increasing and furthering to improve their quality, and value.

In 1989 Dr. Brendell Thomas Francis heard the inward voice of God saying to her, 'I AM THAT I AM placing you in office to serve me better'. And from that definite period she has changed from being that little 6 year old girl who snuck out of her bedroom window during the night. And from that thirteen year old girl who had physically left home to live the street life and yes, it was her decision to leave her parents notably she returned twelve years later. Holy Spirit planned a destiny and a legacy for her life greater than she planned.

Dr Francis's life adhered to divine inspirational utterances given to her by God and those inspirational messages are placed here within *Snippets*.

As her life has hustled her forward God's voice from within her remained constant. She has acquired by experience that God has chosen her as his vessel to influence others that 'I AM THAT I AM' still speaks.

CPSIA information can be obtained
at www.ICGtesting.com
Printed in the USA
LVHW031146070721
691986LV00005B/449